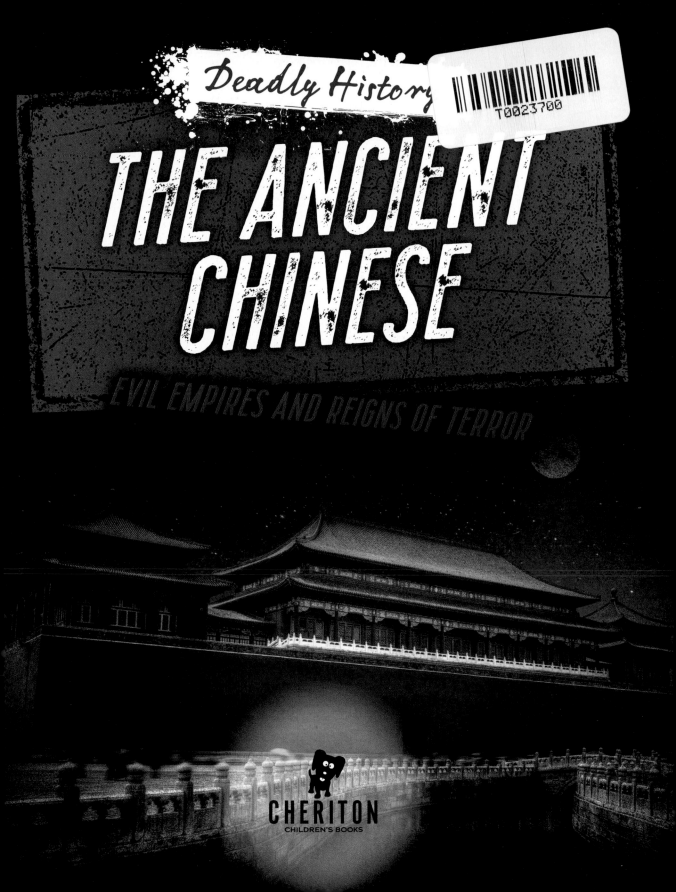

Deadly History

THE ANCIENT CHINESE

EVIL EMPIRES AND REIGNS OF TERROR

CHERITON
CHILDREN'S BOOKS

Published in 2023 by **Cheriton Children's Books**
1 Bank Drive West, Shrewsbury, Shropshire, SY3 9DJ, UK

© 2023 Cheriton Children's Books

First Edition

Authors: Sarah Eason and Louise Spilsbury
Designer: Paul Myerscough
Editor: Deborah Jones
Proofreader: Suzanne Gifford

Printed in China

Please visit our website,
www.cheritonchildrensbooks.com
to see more of our high-quality books.

Glossary 46
Find Out More 47
Index and About the Authors 48

CHAPTER 1

FIERCE FAMILIES

Ancient China was one of the most important **civilizations** in the history of the world. For thousands of years, the country was ruled by a series of powerful families, known as **dynasties**. These dynasties ruled strictly and, often, cruelly.

Deadly Dynasties

The Shang dynasty was the first. Some dynasties had leaders who passed their power to a member of their family when they died. Many dynasties began after a violent battle for power between rival **warlords** or kingdoms. The winner of a war became the new **emperor** and the head of a new dynasty.

Bloody Victory

The Zhou dynasty took over from the Shang after a bloody battle. Zhou emperors told people that their right to rule came from heaven. That made emperors all-powerful and gave them the right to punish or kill anyone who disobeyed them.

Dark and Deadly!

The Shang dynasty rulers were known for **sacrificing** many people. They killed large numbers of prisoners of war and **slaves** in special ceremonies to honor the gods they worshiped.

War Games

The rulers of China's deadly dynasties gained and kept their power using large, bloodthirsty armies that were equipped with lethal weapons.

Chariots Chase

Chariots proved to be a powerful weapon of war. Horse-drawn chariots allowed warriors to chase enemies across the wide, open spaces of ancient China. They could kill opponents from their chariots and take large areas of land under their control.

Deadly Attack

Chinese warriors fired arrows from large bows and hurled long spears with steel tips at enemies in the distance. They launched 10 bolts every 15 seconds from their crossbows. In closer combat, they attacked with **bronze** daggers, battle axes, and doubled-edged swords.

These are the remains of Shang chariots and horses, which were found buried in a grave.

Dark and Deadly!

Ancient Chinese warriors attached special devices to kites. The devices made low, moaning sounds and high-pitched wails in the wind. Enemies hearing these sounds from a kite that they could not see in a foggy sky thought that the gods were angry with them, and ran away.

Ruthless Ruler

For a period of about 250 years, there were endless deadly wars in China because small kingdoms fought each other constantly. This ended in 221 BCE, when the mighty Qin defeated other leaders and became the first emperor of a newly united China.

No Ideas!

Emperor Qin was a ruthless and greatly feared ruler. He ordered all books and writing that went against his ideas to be burned. Anyone found reading such books became a slave or was killed. Some people were buried alive for owning banned books.

China is named for Emperor Qin, which is pronounced "chin". He ruled the country, called China in 221 to 206 BCE.

Keep Out!

Qin began building the Great Wall of China. He forced thousands of prisoners of war, criminals, soldiers, and **peasants** to work on it. Guards prevented anyone from escaping. The wall's final length was 13,000 miles (21,000 km), and it took hundreds of years to build.

Dark and Deadly!

WHY DO YOU THINK QIN WAS DETERMINED TO KEEP PEOPLE FROM READING?

Working conditions were extremely harsh for builders of the Great Wall. More than 100,000 workers died. Many of their bodies were buried under or inside the Wall itself.

The Great Wall of China is one of the most amazing sights on Earth.

CHAPTER 2

EMPIRES OF EVIL

Qin was just the first in a long line of evil emperors. Emperor Yongle ruled from 1402 to 1424. He became known for a type of torture named "death by a thousand cuts."

Cut to Death

Death by a thousand cuts was carried out by cutting off pieces of a victim's flesh over a long period of time. This meant that the person suffered agonizing pain before they died.

Dark and Deadly!

Yongle insisted that people kowtow to him. This is kneeling three times and tapping the forehead against the ground nine times. Anyone who forgot to do this might also have suffered death by a thousand cuts.

Super City

Yongle wanted to own the largest palace complex ever known. More than 1 million workers were forced to drag giant slabs of marble miles across ice from the north to build the Forbidden City. If a stone was damaged, the worker who delivered it could be punished using death by a thousand cuts.

The spectacular Forbidden City has more than 9,000 rooms!

Giant lion statues were created to guard the Forbidden City and terrify all who saw them.

11

Eyes Everywhere

Another emperor, Hongwu, set up the dreaded Jinyi Wei as his personal bodyguards. Later, they were used as a secret police to crush any opposition. The Jinyi Wei were used to watch over officials and root out **rebels**, but these spies were often **corrupt**.

No Fair Trial

Jinyi Wei guards could decide someone was guilty, even if it was a lie. They often demanded money as a bribe to let someone go. Anyone who refused to pay the bribe was put in jail and tortured to death.

People were terrified of the Jinyi Wei.

Dark and Deadly!

Jinyi Wei guards wore a distinctive dragon on their uniform, an ivory tablet on their chest, and carried a special deadly blade. Their tablet gave them the power to arrest, question, and torture anyone they pleased.

WHY DO YOU THINK THE ANCIENT CHINESE RULERS INFLICTED SUCH HORRIBLE PUNISHMENTS ON PEOPLE?

When people saw a guard wearing an ivory tablet like this, they knew he was a Jinyi Wei.

Hacked to Death

Hongwu ordered some people to be killed by **flaying**. Their skin was cut away from their body while they were still alive. The flesh was nailed to a wall as a warning to others not to disobey the horrible Emperor Hongwu.

Monster Mom

Empress Wu is famous for being a ruthless rule-breaker who let no one stand in the way of her rise to power. Wu is accused of killing her own week-old daughter and blaming the baby's death on Wang, the emperor's favorite wife. The emperor believed Wu's story and imprisoned Wang in a distant part of the palace. This made Wu the favorite. After the emperor died, Wu become empress.

Girl Power!

Wu was the only female empress in ancient China's history. She held onto power by keeping her government terrified of what she might do if they crossed her.

A giant statue of Buddha in the Longmen Grottoes in China is believed to have been modeled after the face of Empress Wu.

Dark and Deadly!

Empress Wu got rid of any officials who opposed her rule while she was empress. She fired them, banished them from the kingdom, or had them **executed**.

This statue of Wu shows her as a formidable ruler.

CHAPTER 3

BRUTAL BURIALS

The ancient Chinese believed in an **afterlife**, so they buried items in people's graves to go with them in their next life. They included pots, jewels, and human sacrifices.

An Amazing Woman

Fu Hao was the most powerful woman in the Shang dynasty. She was a great military leader and led the army in great and successful battles against enemies. She was also a priestess who performed ceremonies and sacrifices.

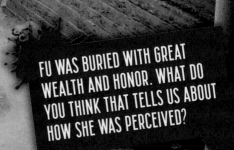

FU WAS BURIED WITH GREAT WEALTH AND HONOR. WHAT DO YOU THINK THAT TELLS US ABOUT HOW SHE WAS PERCEIVED?

Killed to Serve

Fu Hao's grave contained a lot of weapons, jewelry, and shells, which the ancient Chinese used as a form of money. It also contained 16 unfortunate servants who were killed and buried with her, so that they could serve her in the afterlife.

In ancient China, dogs were eaten as food, used for guarding, herding, and hunting, and they were sacrificed to please the gods.

Dark and Deadly!

Six dogs were also sacrificed and buried alongside Fu Hao in the mighty leader's grave. Dog sacrifices were made when tombs were completed. Dogs were often buried to ward off evil spirits or bad luck.

Terrible Tombs

China's early emperors wanted to live forever. They sent officials out on a search across China for potions and herbs that might give them the **immortality** they desired. For example, Emperor Qin swallowed **mercury** because he thought it could prolong his life. However, mercury is deadly poisonous. Qin died on a tour of his empire and officials sneaked him back to the palace with dried fish to disguise the smell of his decaying flesh.

Children Killers

The discovery of some terrible tombs shows that emperors also tried other, more dreadful methods to help them cheat death. At one site **archaeologists** discovered the remains of 113 young children, some as young as two. It is believed they were all sacrificed by an emperor seeking eternal life.

By the time Emperor Qin was buried, his body must have been badly decayed.

Dark and Deadly!

The bodies of the 113 children had been cut up after they were sacrificed. The children's skulls and feet were buried separately, arranged in two small urns made of pottery. The main body parts were buried in a larger urn. Small holes were drilled into the side of the clay coating to let the souls come and go freely.

The grim remains of sacrificed children were put in burial urns like this one.

Eventually, the ancient Chinese made human models and put them in graves rather than sacrificing people.

Dressed for Death

Emperors and other important members of royal families were not only buried with objects they would need when they joined the gods in the afterlife, but some were also covered head to toe in suits made from jade before being buried. Jade is a precious green stone.

This jade suit covers the body of Prince Liu Sheng, who died in 113 BCE.

Dark and Deadly!

Royals thought that jade suits could help them live forever. They hoped that jade would protect the dead from evil spirits and would also keep their dead bodies from decomposing, or rotting.

Magical Stones

The ancient Chinese believed that jade had magical powers. Jade suits contained about 2,000 separate plates of jade. The plates were sewn together around a **corpse** with gold, silver, or bronze wire, depending on how important the dead person was.

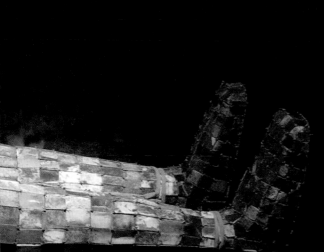

Planning for Death

Royals and **nobles** started planning their burials long before they died because it could take up to 10 years to make a jade suit. A suit encased the body and was shaped to look like a protective suit of armor.

This jade burial suit was sewn together with gold wire. It was very precious.

CHAPTER 4

RELATIVE RAGE!

The ancient Chinese believed that there were many different gods who had power over different parts of their lives. They thought the only way to contact them was through their **ancestors**.

Don't Mess with the Dead!

People carried out **rituals** to honor their ancestors and took good care of their graves. They believed this kept the ancestors happy, who would then ask the gods to bring good luck. If people neglected a dead relative, the ancestor could become a "hungry ghost." They could be very dangerous and do many terrible things.

The ancient Chinese believed in dragon gods, which could control the rain and the sea.

Giving Gifts

To show respect to their ancestors, people left **offerings** of food and wine at grave sites and shrines. These gifts were carried in beautiful containers called ding. The food and wine were meant to help the ancestors survive during the afterlife.

Animals for Honor

During the Shang dynasty, people also sacrificed animals to honor their ancestors. Animals, such as sheep and pigs, were sacrificed in large numbers at ritual ceremonies.

Dark and Deadly!

Ding were elaborate pots made from bronze. The ancient Chinese hoped the offerings inside the ding would help show honor and respect to the ancestors.

A three-legged bronze ding like this one would have been used to make ritual offerings of food and drink to ancestors.

Human Sacrifice

During the Shang dynasty, many human sacrifices were made. Large numbers of people were cruelly murdered in honor of kings and, sometimes, queens. Sacrifices were also made to worship or contact the gods.

Mostly Male

To worship male ancestors such as emperors, the Shang priests chose mostly male victims for sacrifice. The young men were aged between 15 and 35 and came from outside **tribes**. By sacrificing these victims to the ancestors, Shang people hoped to avoid bad luck.

The skeletons of unfortunate victims of cruel sacrifices sometimes reveal the ways in which they were killed.

Dark and Deadly!

The most common method of sacrifice for a male victim during the Shang dynasty was cutting off his head using a dagger or a sacrificial knife. Then the head was offered to the spirits.

Beheading people from different tribes using a sacrificial knife was also a way to scare outsiders into keeping away.

Horrible Deaths

Different methods were used in ritual sacrifices. Victims were beheaded, cut in half, beaten or bled to death, chopped into pieces, buried alive, drowned, or boiled. Burning sacrifices was seen as a way to send the dead, in the form of smoke, up to heaven.

Secrets in the Bones

Some rulers used special oracle bones to find out when would be the best day to offer sacrifices to their ancestors or gods. Oracle bones were usually made from the shoulder blade of an ox. Bones from other animals, such as horses, pigs, and deer, were also used, as well as tortoise shells.

Sawn to Shape

The bone was sawn to shape and shallow pits were drilled into one side. A question was written on the bone in red ink. Hot metal spikes put into the hollow pits caused the bones to crack. If the bone cracked on one side, the answer to the question was "yes." If it cracked on the other, the answer was "no."

Dark and Deadly!

Ancient Chinese rulers asked oracle bones things such as when was the best time to fight a battle and the correct way to perform certain rituals. The oracle bones even told priests how a sacrificial victim should die, so a victim could be beheaded or drowned, depending on the way the oracle bone cracked.

A king's name, the date, the priest's name, the answer, and the number of cracks were all recorded on an oracle bone.

CHAPTER 5

WORKED TO DEATH

While emperors and the royal family lived in luxury and planned their fancy burials, life was hard for ordinary Chinese people. Many of them were worked to death.

Silky Secret

Silk was the most precious fabric in all of ancient China. Many people outside the kingdom of China wanted to buy it and they were willing to pay a very high price for this beautiful cloth. The emperors of China kept the way that silk was made a closely guarded secret.

Moth Killers

Silk is made using the larvae, or caterpillar, of silk moths. The larvae spin silk thread cocoons around themselves when they are ready to transform into moths. Chinese workers steamed the cocoons to kill the moths growing inside, and then removed the threads and spun them together to make silk.

Many thousands of silk moth caterpillars were killed to make silk in ancient China.

Dark and Deadly!

In ancient China, a law stopped workers who made silk from ever revealing how it was done. If a worker was caught stealing silk moth eggs or cocoons, or telling someone how silk was made, they were tortured to death.

A Job to Die For!

Many ordinary people worked on palaces and other huge projects for the power-hungry emperors. It took a hardworking team of around 700,000 workers more than 40 years to build a vast army made from a type of clay, called terracotta, for Emperor Qin. It was the last job they would ever do.

Fighting Forever

The 8,000 life-size soldiers are buried near Emperor Qin's tomb. They were made to protect him in the afterlife.

Each soldier is thought to have been based on real soldiers who served in the emperor's army.

Murdered Workers

The location of Qin's tomb was a well-kept secret, for fear people might steal its treasures. Many people believe that when the army was completed, the workers were all murdered so that they could never reveal its location.

Dark and Deadly!

Qin's actual tomb is about 130 feet (40 m) underground. It has not yet been opened because it is surrounded by deadly mercury and archaeologists worry it may be booby-trapped.

WHY DO YOU THINK QIN WAS SO DETERMINED TO KEEP HIS TOMB A SECRET?

As well as soldiers, there are also clay horses and chariots in the incredible Terracotta Army, which was not discovered until 1974.

Suffering Slaves

The lives of the slaves were the hardest of all, and they were given the most horrible jobs. Slaves had to do any job they were told to, without any payment. They had to work hard for their masters and were treated with great cruelty.

These are statues of house slaves. Many rich people kept house slaves to show their wealth and importance.

Dark and Deadly!

When a slave's owner died, the slave was killed or even buried alive with their master in his tomb. This was so the slave could continue to serve him in the afterlife.

Forced into Slavery

Some people were forced to become slaves if their relative was a criminal condemned to death. Also, when an emperor's army defeated an enemy, the army captured prisoners, who were then made into slaves.

Horrible Work

Slaves built palaces, dug tombs, constructed roads and bridges, cut trees for wood timber, and worked in mines, digging for metals such as copper. Poor slaves also sweated by large fires to make tools and over pans of boiling seawater to get salt.

Figurines of slaves have also been found buried in tombs.

CHAPTER 6

HIDEOUS HABITS

The ancient Chinese had many horrible habits. They ranged from wearing foot bindings and macabre makeup to eating awful meals.

Tiny Feet

The ancient Chinese thought tiny feet were beautiful. Tiny feet also ensured young girls sat still often and helped make goods such as cloth, mats, and fishing nets for families to sell.

Broken and Bound

To make sure a girl's feet were kept tiny, at a young age, the toes on her feet were broken and folded under her feet. The foot arches were bent double and were strapped tightly and painfully into place by a long silk strip.

Dark and Deadly!

Once bound, over the next two years, the straps were only briefly removed to clean blood and pus, and to cut away excess flesh. After that, the feet were crushed permanently together and were tiny.

Deadly Makeup

In ancient China, women went to great lengths to make themselves look beautiful. Women had little power, so one reason they wore makeup was to attract a husband. Their tiny feet and luxurious silk robes also showed off the family's wealth and importance.

Far from Fabulous!

The ingredients used in makeup were truly horrible. Women in ancient China colored their lips with a paste made from the leaves of red and blue flowering plants mixed with oil or fat from cows and pigs. They decorated their cheeks and forehead by gluing on fish scales, bird feathers, and dragonfly wings.

In ancient China, white skin, red cheeks, and large red lips were fashionable.

Dark and Deadly!

To stick flower petals and other decorative items to their cheeks, ancient Chinese women often used fish guts as a strange, and probably very smelly, type of glue.

Eaten Alive

Women shaved their eyebrows and painted on new ones using soot from burned willow branches. To make the face look whiter, some women used a mixture of vinegar and lead. Unfortunately, over time, the lead ate away the skin, causing painful scars.

A makeup box like this could have held a mirror, rouge for cheeks, and lipstick.

Foul Feasting

In ancient China, most people ate quite a healthy diet with a lot of rice and vegetables. However, some of the dishes on the dinner menu at a feast were disgusting.

Hard-Boiled Urine

One specialty was urine eggs. These were just as you would imagine from the name. Eggs were boiled for an entire day in the urine of boys under the age of 10. The ancient Chinese thought these eggs were very good for their health.

Delicious or Disgusting?

Bears' paws, camels' humps, apes' lips, rhinoceroses' tails, and sharks' fins were considered **delicacies** at feasts and festivals. During the Han dynasty, monkey brains were very popular. **Legend** has it that in the past, diners spooned fresh brains out of a monkey's skull while it was still alive.

Dark and Deadly!

The Zhou emperor sent hunters into central China to kill wild elephants. He ordered them to cut off each elephant's two large teeth, called tusks, so he could eat his meals using special ivory chopsticks.

Ivory chopsticks are carved from an elephant's tusks.

Sharks were hunted and killed for their fins, which were prized by the ancient Chinese.

Ancient Recyclers

Ancient Chinese farmers were among the first recyclers. They never threw anything away that could be useful —they even made use of their toilet waste.

Toilet Treasures

In early China, human **feces** were collected from public toilets and sold to farmers. The farmers spread this human waste, known as "night-soil," on their fields to act as cheap fertilizer. Collecting feces was such a good way to earn money in ancient China that there was even a saying about it: "Treasure night-soil as if it were gold."

Poop for Pigs!

Some farmers in ancient China built a special type of outbuilding above the pen where they kept their pigs. They built a room over the pen that they used as a bathroom so their feces would fall directly into the pigs' trough below. For the pigs in the pen beneath them, this was their dinner.

Dark and Deadly!

Toilet paper was one of ancient China's many great inventions, but only the emperors were allowed to use it. Some other people wiped themselves clean with a bamboo stick that had a strip of fabric wound around it.

Spreading human waste onto terraces like these to fertilize crops must have

Amazing Acupuncture

The ancient Chinese had some wacky ways of treating illness, but some of them really worked. Acupuncture is an ancient Chinese treatment that involves sticking needles into certain points of the body. Like many other Chinese inventions and discoveries, acupuncture works and is still used today all over the world to ease pain and prevent illness.

This model shows the acupuncture points, or places to put needles, for the front of the head.

Nasty Medicines

During the early dynasties, people thought illnesses were caused by evil spirits. They chanted spells and ate crushed **fossils**, which they thought were dragon bones, for cures.

Sickening Soup

To cure **diarrhea**, ancient Chinese doctors recommended eating a yellow soup. It smelled and tasted awful because it contained feces from a healthy person, but it worked!

Dark and Deadly!

A talisman was an object with writing on it that the ancient Chinese believed held magical powers. Some people believed burning a talisman and swallowing the ashes in water cured diseases.

It's easy to understand why the ancient Chinese believed dinosaur fossils were dragons when you look at the bones of a T. rex.

END OF THE EMPIRE

The last ancient Chinese dynasty was the Han dynasty. The Han dynasty ended in 220 CE. Many people believe that the era of Chinese dynasties ended much as it had begun, in blood and violence.

By the Han dynasty, people were tired of paying for emperors' luxuries, including tombs filled with treasure such as this statue.

Death and Disaster

The final years of the Han dynasty were plagued with natural disasters, and one Han emperor after another died young or without an **heir**. Ordinary people started to think that these events were signs that the gods were unhappy with their leaders.

Fighting Families

Fights for control broke out between members of the ruling families, and peasants started to rebel against their leaders. Then a warlord named Dong Zhou took control of the country. By 220 CE, the last emperor was gone and the Han dynasty was finally over.

This is a model of a Han warrior. These soldiers were unable to defeat the warlords who finally overran the ancient Chinese Empire.

Dark and Deadly!

After 220 CE, China was ripped apart by deadly wars between different regions. It was hundreds of years before China was a united country again.

GLOSSARY

afterlife life after death. Some people believe that after we die we go to live in another world

ancestors relatives who have died

archaeologists people who study objects to learn about how people lived in the past

beheading killing a person by cutting off their head

bronze a metal made from a mixture of melted metals

civilizations settled communities in which people live together and use systems such as writing to communicate

corpse a dead body

corrupt doing things that are dishonest or illegal in order to make money or to gain or keep power

delicacies things that are pleasing to eat or that are rare or luxurious

diarrhea a condition that involves unusually frequent and liquid bowel movements

dynasties families that rule countries for a long time, because after leaders die, their eldest sons take over

emperor a male leader or ruler of an empire

executed killed on someone's orders

feces digestive waste

flaying stripping off the skin

fossils remains of dead plants and animals from millions of years ago

heir someone who inherits or is entitled to become the next ruler

immortality the ability to live forever

legend a very old story from ancient times that is not always true

mercury a silvery-white metal

nobles people in the highest classes in certain societies

offering something that people give as part of a religious ceremony or ritual

peasants uneducated people who are often the lowest rank in society

rebels people who oppose or fight those in power

rituals ceremonies performed for religious reasons

sacrificing killing to honor a god or gods

slaves people who are owned by another person and have to obey them

tribes groups of people who live together, sharing the same language, culture, and history

warlords military leaders of a warlike region

FIND OUT MORE

Books

Faust, Daniel R. *Ancient China* (Look at Ancient Civilizations).
Gareth Stevens Publishing, 2019.

Randolph, Joanne. *Living and Working in Ancient China* (Back in Time).
Enslow Publishing, 2017.

Spilsbury, Louise. *Ancient China* (Analyze the Ancients).
Gareth Stevens Publishing, 2018.

Websites

This website has a lot of details about ancient China:
https://china.mrdonn.org

Learn more about ancient China at:
www.dkfindout.com/us/history/ancient-china

Find extra information about early China at:
www.ducksters.com/history/china/ancient_china.php

Publisher's note to educators and parents:
All the websites featured above have been carefully reviewed to ensure
that they are suitable for students. However, many websites change often,
and we cannot guarantee that a site's future contents will continue to
meet our high standards of educational value. Please be advised that
students should be closely monitored whenever they access the Internet.

INDEX

afterlife 16, 17, 20, 23, 30, 32
ancestors 22, 23, 24, 26
armies 4, 6, 16, 30, 31, 33

battles 4, 6, 7, 16, 26, 27
books 8
burials 6, 8, 9, 16, 17, 18, 19, 20, 21, 25, 28, 30, 32

chariots 6, 31

dogs 17
dynasties 4, 6, 23, 43, 44
    Han 38, 44, 45
    Shang 4, 5, 16, 24, 25
    Zhou 4

emperors 4, 8, 10, 12, 13, 14, 18, 20, 24, 28, 30, 33, 39, 41, 44, 45
Empress Wu 14, 15

feasts 38
flaying 13
foot binding 34
Forbidden City 11
Fu Hao 16, 17

gods 5, 7, 17, 20, 22, 24, 26, 45
graves 6, 16, 17, 19, 22, 23
Great Wall of China 9

jade 20, 21

kites 7

makeup 34, 36, 37
medicines 42

oracle bones 26, 27

palaces 11, 14, 18, 30, 33

rituals 23, 24, 25, 27

sacrifice 16, 17, 18, 19, 23, 24, 25, 26
silk 28, 29, 35, 36
slaves 5, 8, 32, 33
spies 12

toilets 40, 41
tombs 16, 17, 18, 30, 31, 33, 44
torture 10, 12, 13, 29

warriors 6, 7, 45
weapons 6, 7

About the Authors

Sarah Eason and Louise Spilsbury have written many history books for children. Both love finding out about past people, and through writing this book have learned how deadly daily life really was for people who lived during the age of the chilling ancient Chinese.